NOW YOU SEE IT...

The Incredible Illusions of Ethan Flask and Professor von Offel

MAD SCIENCE

by Anne Capeci
Creative development by Gordon Korman

SCHOLASTIC INC.
New York   Toronto   London   Auckland   Sydney
Mexico City   New Delhi   Hong Kong

NOW YOU SEE IT . . .
The Incredible Illusions of Ethan Flask and Professor von Offel

ISBN 0-439-22857-3

Published by Scholastic Inc., 555 Broadway, New York, NY 10012.

Mad Science®: Registered trademark of the Mad Science Group used under license by Scholastic Inc.

SCHOLASTIC and associated logos are trademarks and/or registered trademarks of Scholastic Inc.

12 11 10 9 8 7 6 5 4 3 2   1 2 3 4 5/0

Printed in the U.S.A.   40

First Scholastic printing, November 2000

NOW YOU
SEE IT...

Table of Contents

Prologue

For more than 100 years, the Flasks, the town of Arcana's first family of science, have been methodically, precisely, safely, in other words, *scientifically* inventing all kinds of things.

For more than 100 years, the von Offels, Arcana's first family of sneaks, have been stealing those inventions.

Where the Flasks are brilliant, rational, and reliable, the von Offels are brilliant, reckless, and ruthless. The nearly fabulous Flasks could have earned themselves a major chapter in the history of science — but at every key moment, there has always seemed to be a von Offel on the scene to "borrow" a science notebook, beat a Flask to the punch on a patent, or booby-trap an important experiment. Just take a look at the Flask family tree and then the von Offel clan. Coincidence? Or *evidence*!

Despite being tricked out of fame and fortune by the awful von Offels, the Flasks doggedly continued their scientific inquiries. The last of the family line, Ethan Flask, is no exception. An outstanding sixth-grade science teacher, he's also conducting studies into animal intelligence and is competing for the Third Millennium Foundation's pretigious Vanguard Teacher Award. Unfortunately, the person who's evaluating Ethan for the award is none other than Professor John von Offel, a.k.a., the original mad scientist, Johannes von Offel.

Von Offel needs a Flask to help him regain the body he lost in an explosive experiment so many decades ago. When last seen in *What a Blast!, The Explosive Escapades of Ethan Flask and Professor von Offel*, the professor's most recent effort had just failed miserably — unless you call exploding a 270-pound watermelon at a PTA meeting a success!

And that's not all: Flask's lab assistants are

suspicious about the Professor's true identity: His parrot, Atom, has become too chatty (and is being overheard by the wrong ears), and von Offel doesn't yet see how Flask's unit on tricks and optical illusions is going to help him.

But a von Offel can be pretty tricky himself. . . .

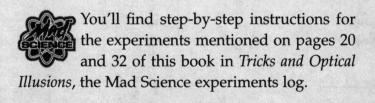 You'll find step-by-step instructions for the experiments mentioned on pages 20 and 32 of this book in *Tricks and Optical Illusions*, the Mad Science experiments log.

The Nearly-Fabulous Flasks

Jedidiah Flask
2nd person to create rubber band

Oliver Flask
Missed appointment to patent new glue because he was mysteriously epoxied to his chair

Augustus Flask
Developed telephone; got a busy signal

Mildred Flask Tachyon
Tranquilizer formula never registered; carriage horses fell asleep en route to patent office

Lane Tachyon
Developed laughing gas; was kept in hysterics while a burglar stole the formula

Percy Flask
Lost notes on cure for common cold in pick-pocketing incident

Marlow Flask
Runner-up to Adolphus von Offel for Sir Isaac Newton Science Prize

Archibald Flask
Knocked out cold en route to patent superior baseball bat

Amaryllis Flask Lepton
Discovered new kind of amoeba; never published findings due to dysentery

Norton Flask
Clubbed with seven-minute gray meat loaf and robbed of prototype microwave oven

Salome Flask Rhombus
Discovered cloud-salting with dry ice; never made it to patent office due to freak downpour

Constance Rhombus Ampère
Lost Marie Curie Award to Beatrice O'Door; voted Miss Congeniality

Roland Flask
His new high-speed engine was believed to have powered the getaway car that stole his prototype

Michael Flask
Arrived with gas grill schematic only to find tailgate party outside patent office

Solomon Ampère
Bionic horse placed in Kentucky Derby after von Offel entry

Margaret Flask Geiger
Name was mysteriously deleted from registration papers for her undetectable correction fluid

Ethan Flask

The Awful von Offels

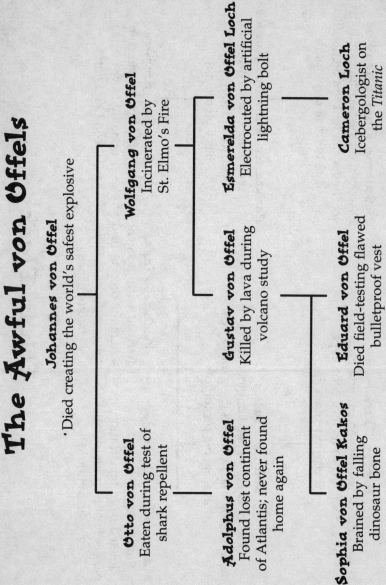

Johannes von Offel
Died creating the world's safest explosive

Wolfgang von Offel
Incinerated by
St. Elmo's Fire

Esmerelda von Offel Loch
Electrocuted by artificial
lightning bolt

Cameron Loch
Icebergologist on
the *Titanic*

Gustav von Offel
Killed by lava during
volcano study

Eduard von Offel
Died field-testing flawed
bulletproof vest

Otto von Offel
Eaten during test of
shark repellent

Adolphus von Offel
Found lost continent
of Atlantis; never found
home again

Sophia von Offel Kakos
Brained by falling
dinosaur bone

Kurt von Offel
Weak batteries in antigravity backpack

Colin von Offel
Transplanted his brain into wildebeest

Felicity von Offel Day
Brained by diving bell during deep-sea exploration

Alan von Offel
Failed to survive field test of nonpoisonous arsenic

Bula von Offel Malle
Evaporated

Beatrice Malle O'Door
Drowned pursuing the Loch Ness Monster

Feldspar O'Door
Died of freezer burn during cryogenics experiment

Professor John von Offel (?)

Johannes von Offel's
Book of Scientific Observations,
1891

The shrub-pruning pact was one of the most profitable endeavors I entered into with my neighbor and colleague, Jedidiah Flask. He would trim my bushes when I was away, and I would do the same for him. To make it official, I drafted a letter for us both to sign. Three days later, I presented that same letter at the United States Patent Office in Washington, D.C. Only now it stated that Jedidiah was transferring full ownership of his (or should I say my?) latest invention, the steam-powered walking stick. Jedidiah cried foul, but I say a true scientist should have noticed the disappearing ink on the letter he signed. All science is observation, but the eye and the brain can be tricked.

CHAPTER 1

Secrets of a Mad Scientist

"Look," said Luis Antilla. He jogged past his two best friends, Alberta Wong and Prescott Forrester III. They rolled along on in-line skates, trying to keep up. "Mr. Flask deserves the Vanguard Teacher Award." Luis turned and jogged backward, facing his friends. "The only roadblock to him winning it is that awful Professor von Offel."

"You are the roadblock around here." Alberta laughed.

"Watch out!" Prescott said. "Once I start rolling, I can't stop. Whoa!"

Alberta grabbed Prescott to steady him. "Listen, you guys," she said. "Just because the Flasks and the von Offels haven't always seen eye to eye doesn't mean the professor won't be scrupulous. He's bound to see how great Mr. Flask is!"

Luis's eyebrows shot up. "*Scrupulous?* I don't think any von Offel knows what the word means! They were too busy stealing major scientific breakthroughs from the Flasks to look it up in the dictionary."

"Did someone call my name?"

Ethan Flask whizzed past all three kids on his bicycle built for two. Harnessed to his shoulders was a video camera aimed at the passenger on the bike's rear seat — a blindfolded orangutan.

"Mr. Flask! Hi!" Alberta called, waving. "Hi, Uri!"

Mr. Flask smiled and waved back, then steered the bike around a corner. The last thing the sixth graders saw was the orangutan pounding away at its chest.

"Think about it," Luis said. "Mr. Flask would be rich today if all those von Offels hadn't cheated his family out of the royalties from their inventions."

"I don't think Mr. Flask cares whether he's rich or not," said Prescott. "Just so long as he gets to keep working on his animal intelligence studies."

"Besides, maybe this time a von Offel can help a Flask," Alberta said.

"What do you mean?" asked Luis.

"Well," Alberta said, "I'm sure the professor must be working on some project of his own."

"You mean, apart from evaluating Mr. Flask for the award?" Prescott asked.

Alberta nodded. "He's got to be! Science is in his genes. If we can find out what the professor is working on, we could tell Mr. Flask. Then he could do something scientific to help the professor, and *ta-da*! Mr. Flask makes a good impression, Mr. Flask becomes Vanguard Teacher of the Year."

"Makes sense," Luis agreed.

"I'm game," said Prescott.

"Good." Alberta nodded. "From now on our mission is to discover anything we can about Professor von Offel's private work."

CHAPTER 2

Shadow of a Doubt

"On with the show!" Professor John von Offel said under his breath. He pulled open the front door to Einstein Elementary School and stepped inside.

Wild tufts of hair shot out from his head like lightning bolts. He moved so fast that the battered green parrot perched on his shoulder had trouble keeping its balance.

"Slow down!" squawked the parrot.

"Time is of the essence, Atom!" the professor said. "We have yet to purloin — er, learn — the secret of my recovery from young Ethan Flask."

"We?" the parrot echoed. "I'm not the one who blew himself into oblivion. Plus, you burned my tail feathers! A hundred and ten years I've been waiting for them to grow back. "

"Quiet, my little feathered megaphone!" Professor von Offel glanced left and right. "No one here suspects my true identity."

"You mean that you're really the wacko Johannes von Offel who's been trying to conjure his body

4

back into reality after your explosive mishap more than a century ago?" Atom scoffed.

The professor puffed himself up. "I'm here, am I not? A man of flesh and blood." He thumped himself on the chest and immediately started coughing. He turned to Atom with eyes that faded in and out of focus. "Well, almost."

"Sixty-five percent here, to be exact," Atom squawked. "You're lucky anyone can see you at all. A gust of wind has more substance than you do. Not even your clothes have fully materialized through and through. You don't even cast a shadow!"

"Ethan Flask will help me change all that," Professor von Offel said. "That twit will unwittingly reveal the secret of full corporeality, just as all the Flasks have lost their best ideas to the von Offels. It's simply a matter of —"

"Professor von Offel!" A high-pitched voice sailed through the air, setting the professor's teeth on edge. He looked up to see Mrs. Ratner, the president of the PTA, making a beeline for him in her high heels and pale green suit.

"What can that old bat want?" he muttered.

"How good of you to come, Professor!" Mrs. Ratner gushed, taking his arm and leading him down the hall. "We certainly can use all the help we can get setting up our annual book fair."

"Book fair?" Professor von Offel looked toward the gym and frowned. Inside, several other parents hovered around trunklike cases on wheels. "The term is unfamiliar, madam. In any case, I'm afraid I can't . . ."

Mrs. Ratner was already hustling the professor through the doorway. "I knew you wouldn't disappoint us. A strong man like you is just what we need to move these portable display cases into place."

Atom gave a series of loud, chortling squawks. The bird laughed so hard he nearly rolled off the professor's shoulder.

"Is your pet all right?" asked Mrs. Ratner.

"It's probably just some dust lodged in his throat." The professor whacked Atom on the back.

"Ouch! I mean, awk!" the parrot cried.

"Well!" Mrs. Ratner said. She led the professor over to two men who were rolling the portable cases into rows. "I'm sure you've met Mr. Kondrakos, the sixth-grade English teacher."

The older of the two men straightened up and held out his hand. "I've been looking forward to the honor, Professor. It's a pleasure to finally meet a colleague of my own generation," he droned in a flat voice. "Someone who understands the value of a rigorous educational training in the traditional sense."

"Tradition. Yes," the professor said. "Well, I can't really . . ."

He tried to pull away, but Mrs. Ratner had his arm in a viselike grip. She pushed him over to the second man, a dough-faced teacher with red hair and boyish eyes.

"This is Mr. Delaney, our social studies teacher," Mrs. Ratner went on. "He hasn't been here quite as long as Mr. Kondrakos."

"Forty-two years this fall," Mr. Kondrakos announced, proudly straightening his tweed suit.

"We'll show you the ropes, Professor von Offel," Mr. Delaney offered. "You can start by helping those two PTA ladies over there arrange these books after Mr. Kondrakos and I get this bookcase into place."

The professor, wedged in between the rolling bookcase and Mrs. Ratner, had no choice. The next thing he knew he was standing next to the bookcase in the sunlight near the windows.

"There we go," said Mr. Delaney, opening up the case.

The professor reached for one of the books. He flexed it first to one side, then to the other.

"Fascinating!" he exclaimed. "I've never seen such a thing. I thought all such volumes were leather-bound."

"Shhhh!" hissed Atom.

"You've never seen a paperback book?" Mrs. Ratner raised her eyebrows and then laughed nervously. "But, of course, you're joking, Professor. I never knew you had such a sense of hu —"

She broke off suddenly and stared at the wall behind Professor von Offel as if a three-headed monster had suddenly appeared there.

"Is there a problem, madam?" the professor inquired.

"The sh-sh-shadows." Mrs. Ratner pointed in turn at Professor von Offel, Mr. Kondrakos, Mr. Delaney, and the two PTA women. "There are only four of them, but there are five of you!"

"Uh-oh," Atom said.

The parrot pushed the professor away from the sunlit windows with his flapping wings. "Scram!" he screeched.

"How odd!" Mrs. Ratner said, still staring at the wall. "Your parrot was perched on your shoulder, Professor. Yet I could have sworn his shadow was suspended by itself."

"Awk!" Atom dive-bombed Mrs. Ratner's perfectly coiffed head. She dived for cover behind one of the bookcases.

"Atom!" the professor scolded. But the corners of his mouth twitched into a near smile. He turned to the PTA president. "Surely your eyes played tricks on you, Mrs. Ratner."

"I saw the same thing," one of the other women piped up. She eyed Atom nervously as he circled overhead.

"An optical illusion, no more, ladies," Professor von Offel insisted. He paced back and forth, keeping well out of the sun's rays. "Such phenomena occur when the angle of projection of the sun's rays is perpendicular to the path created by the optic nerve, with an inverse relationship to light's speed. Thus, rays of light moving in opposite directions appear to cancel each other out, when in reality no such thing has taken place."

Mrs. Ratner's eyes glazed over. She had to shake herself a few times before she could speak.

"I know what I saw, Professor," she said, then ducked as Atom shot toward her again. "Anyway, if it was an illusion, we'll know soon enough. That bird can't keep flying forever."

Atom swooped close to the professor. "What now, Einstein?" he asked, masking his voice with his flapping wings.

The professor nodded toward the heavy glass windowpanes. "Accident!" he hissed.

The parrot took one look, then shook his head. He stayed where he was, hovering over the professor's head.

Professor von Offel's eyes bulged from their sockets. "Now!"

With a deep sigh, Atom flapped his wings and picked up speed. "I must be crazy," he said. Then he flew straight toward one of the windows.

Wham!

The parrot struck the glass beak-first, then plummeted to the floor.

"The poor thing!" gasped Mrs. Ratner.

Professor von Offel pounced on the stunned bird. He picked up Atom and ran for the door.

"This bird needs a doctor!" he bellowed. "I mean, a veterinarian!"

CHAPTER 3

Now You See It . . .

"Oh, my beak! My aching beak!" Atom groaned.

"Shhh!" Professor von Offel ran into the sixth-grade science lab; the parrot was cupped in his hands. As he dropped Atom onto the experiment table at the front of the classroom, a chorus of animal hisses, coos, and buzzes sounded from the cages scattered throughout the room.

"Ohhhh." The dazed parrot took a few stumbling steps. "I hope you appreciated my little show."

"I can't believe those witches fell for the oldest trick in the book!" the professor crowed. "Still —" He clasped his hands behind his back. "They're onto us. How can we throw them off the scent?"

"Oh, no. Not me. I've had it with your tricks," Atom squawked. "Why can't you be a normal scientist? I'll bet my singed tail feathers Ethan Flask wouldn't spout the kinds of phony scientific jargon you pull out of your hat. Light rays canceling each other out, ha!"

"Flask wouldn't have the nerve!" scoffed the professor. "He isn't half the man I am."

His last word faded into a wheezing cough.

"I rest my case," Atom said.

"Shhh!" warned the professor, turning toward the doorway. "Do you hear that?"

Mr. Klumpp's angry voice shrilled just outside the classroom.

"You've cheated me, Mr. Flask! I put a ten-dollar bill in that box, and now it's gone!"

"Calm down, Mr. Klumpp," Ethan Flask reassured the school custodian. "This is an Illusion Box. Mirrors make it look as if your money is gone, but it's really right here. See?"

"Young Flask!" said the professor. "Atom, we must be alert for the inspiration that will bring me all the way back into this world!"

The sound of a wallet snapping closed came from the hallway.

"I don't like being tricked," snorted the custodian.

"No harm intended, I assure you, Mr. Klumpp," Ethan said. "I'm just testing out my new science unit on tricks and optical illusions. We'll be starting it in class today."

"Optical illusions, eh?" Professor von Offel's vague eyes flashed. "There may be something in this for us, Atom!"

"Count me out, Prof." The parrot flew away from von Offel and landed on a coatrack.

The coatrack jerked forward three feet — on its own.

"Yikes!" the parrot cried. "What —?"

He looked down and saw two long, hairy, apelike arms dangling from the coatrack. An orangutan stared up at the flustered bird.

"Another one of Flask's ridiculous beasts," the professor said with a wave of his hand. "Animal intelligence. What an absurd field of study!" He pulled his hand down quickly. Another second and it would have been skewered by Atom's sharp beak.

Atom then jumped off the coatrack as the orangutan swung toward him with an unfriendly grunt. "Keep away, you baboon!" the parrot screeched.

He darted into the air. Atom was so busy keeping his eyes on the hairy creature that he didn't see the windows looming in front of him — until it was too late.

He bounced off the glass and landed on one of the desks.

"Ohhhh. When will I ever learn?"

CHAPTER 4

Going Ape

"Ah, marvelous! I see you've met Uri, Professor von Offel." Ethan walked into the science lab, his arms and lab coat pockets loaded with tubes, mirrors, and 3-D glasses.

"Er, yes. Unfortunately." The professor shrank away from the orangutan, which was sniffing the quill pen and inkwell the professor had just placed on his desk. "Can't you control this animal pest?"

Atom circled overhead and echoed, "Animal pest! Awk!"

"Be right there, Professor," Ethan called. He turned behind him to Mr. Klumpp, who followed, carrying a poster, a stack of cups, and a cardboard box with mirrors glued inside it at different angles. "Thank you for helping me with these supplies, Mr. Klumpp. I hope there are no hard feelings about the Illusion Box."

The custodian snorted as he plunked the equipment down on the experiment table. "I suppose you'll be needing me to clean up after —" He glowered in the direction of the cages scattered throughout the lab.

"Mr. Flask!" Professor von Offel glared impatiently at the orangutan.

"I can help you, Professor!" Alberta was at the professor's elbow a nanosecond after she entered the room.

Behind her, Luis, Prescott, and several other students trickled in.

"You would think she's the one up for the Vanguard Teacher Award," Luis whispered as Alberta steered Uri away from the professor.

"Well, if we want Mr. Flask to impress Professor von Offel, then we should help, too, right?" Prescott said to Luis. "Anyway, aren't we supposed to be figuring out what kinds of private projects the professor has going?"

"You must be so busy, Professor," Alberta was saying, "between your job for the Millennium Foundation and your own very important scientific work."

Luis and Prescott inched closer; they were all ears.

"A bright light like myself does keep busy," the professor began.

"I'd love to hear more about what you're working on, Professor," Alberta gushed.

The professor opened his mouth, then snapped it shut when Atom let out a squawk in his ear.

"I — uh — young lady, my private scientific studies are neither your concern nor within the realm of your comprehension," he said sternly.

At the front of the room, Ethan watched the professor's face closely. "Let's leave the professor to do his job, shall we, Alberta? Settle down, everyone."

"Check out that dumb monkey." Sean Baxter's loud voice sounded from the doorway.

"Actually, orangutans are apes, a different species of primate altogether from the monkey," Mr. Flask said. "And for your information, Sean, orangutans are quite smart. They can make and use tools. Some studies show they can reason out solutions to problems much the same way people do."

"He's so cute," Heather Patterson cooed. "Can I feed him?"

Luis, Prescott, Sean, Max Hoof, and half a dozen other boys dived for the shelf where the animals' food was stored.

"The dried mangos are Uri's favorite," Luis said. He held the plastic container out to Heather with a goofy smile that made Alberta shake her head with disgust. There was no scientific explanation for it. For some reason, boys turned into complete morons around Heather.

"Mr. Flask, you've gone too far!" Mr. Klumpp cried as Uri swung over to investigate the pile of wood shavings he was sweeping up near the cages. The custodian jumped back, sending the shavings flying into the air like confetti.

15

"That wild beast has no place in the classroom," he seethed. "It's not safe!"

"Uri is quite docile, Mr. Klumpp," Ethan assured him. "Besides, we're not studying Uri at the moment. Our next unit is on tricks and optical illusions, as I told you, and they've never hurt anyone."

Mr. Klumpp refused to back off. "This isn't a zoo," he insisted. "This is a school."

"Exactly my point!" Ethan agreed. "My students have the chance to see important fieldwork. I'm evaluating Uri's ability to recognize and remember individual humans."

Alberta leaned close to Luis's desk and whispered, "That should score points with Professor von Offel."

At the back of the room, the professor chuckled. "What utter nonsense!" he scoffed. He pulled a rusted monocle from his shirt pocket and stared through the lens at the orangutan. "A dumb ape has nothing close to the smarts necessary to distinguish between individuals."

"Yeah! Dumb ape! Dumb ape!" Atom screeched. He shot higher in the air as Uri's arm swung wildly toward him. "I mean — awk!"

"Not necessarily," Ethan countered. "For example, if Uri were confronted with a female that was ready to mate, he would take specific notice of her by giving this mating call."

Ethan began beating the front of his lab coat with

16

his fists. He let loose a yodel that made everyone in the room cover their ears.

"You sound like a beached whale, Mr. Flask!" Preston said, choking back a laugh.

"Look at Uri!" Alberta cried.

The orangutan was rolling on his back, slapping the floor. He looked like he was laughing. Everyone in the classroom started roaring.

Everyone except Mr. Klumpp, Atom, and Professor von Offel.

"Perhaps I don't have the call quite right yet," Ethan admitted sheepishly. "Still, you get the idea. Uri has a specific call for a specific female. I think it's quite possible that he can distinguish between people, too."

"Are you arguing with me?" the professor asked.

Ethan hesitated for half a second before answering. "Surely you support the open exchange of scientific ideas," he said.

"You may be forgetting, sir," said the professor, glaring through his monocle at Ethan, "that *I* am the one evaluating *you* for the Vanguard Teacher Award."

CHAPTER 5

Elusive Illusions

"So much for scoring points," Prescott said.

"Mr. Flask?" Luis's hand shot into the air. "Should we assistants set up the materials for today's experiments?"

"Yes. Absolutely," Ethan said. He seemed grateful for a reason to escape the professor's critical gaze. "Let's get started, class."

Mr. Flask's enthusiasm spread through the room. Kids leaned forward. Curious comments were called out from all corners as Alberta, Prescott, and Luis sifted through the things on the front table.

"How are tubes optical illusions?" Heather asked.

"Could I try on those 3-D glasses?" someone else called out.

"What are those cups for?" Max wanted to know. "I really prefer to drink out of glasses."

"The cups aren't for drinking, Max. We'll be getting to the actual experiments in a minute. But first" — Ethan leaned against the table, crossed his arms over the front of his lab coat, and asked — "who knows what an optical illusion is?"

Heather raised her hand. "Something that isn't really there?"

"A mirage is something that isn't really there," Ethan explained. "But you're on the right track, Heather. Optical illusions have to do with the ways our eyes perceive images."

"What's the big deal about that?" said Sean. "Something is there. You see it. End of story."

"It's a little more complicated than that," Ethan chuckled. "We can see things because light waves bounce off objects in the world around us and then register those images on the photoreceptor cells on the retina of the eye."

"So light waves send a kind of photographic picture to our eyes," Luis said. "And that's what we see as the world around us."

Ethan nodded. "Excellent!" he said. "What's interesting is that the images imprinted on the eye are flat. Yet somehow we perceive a three-dimensional world, complete with all its wonderful depth and motion."

Alberta glanced toward the back of the classroom, where Professor von Offel sat hunched over his desk, scratching at his paper with his quill pen. "I think he's really impressed," she whispered to Luis and Prescott. "Don't you?"

Prescott shrugged. "At least there isn't steam coming out of his ears anymore."

"So where do the illusions come in?" Max asked.

"Well, every flat image can have more than one

19

three-dimensional interpretation," Ethan explained. "Usually, we make the correct interpretation because our brain knows what to expect. But if we confront the eye with visual information the brain isn't expecting, the results can be very . . . interesting."

Sean didn't look convinced. "Like what?" he asked.

Mr. Flask picked up a rolled poster that lay on the experiment table. "A riddle: When is a rabbit not a rabbit?" He taped the poster to the chalkboard. "Answer: When it's a duck. Look at this picture closely. There's only one image, but if you look closely, you'll see both animals."

Mr. Klumpp finished dumping the last of the wood shavings from the cages into the trash bin. Halfway to the door, he stopped in his tracks and stared at the poster.

"Wait a minute," he said. "There's no rabbit, there's just a duck. Look at its bill."

"That's what I see, too," said Alberta.

Mr. Flask's mouth curved in a mysterious smile. "Are you sure? Look closely, everyone."

Twenty pairs of eyes squinted at the poster. Professor von Offel peered through his monocle. Atom covered one eye with his wing and stared at the poster with the other. Uri tilted his head to the side, a leathery hand over his left eye.

Keeping his eyes glued to the poster, Mr. Klumpp stepped forward and then back.

"Bah!" he said, shaking his head. "You can't fool me. There is no bunny, just a quacker."

"I see her!" Alberta crowed, sitting bolt upright. "The duck's bill turns into the rabbit's ears."

"Yeah. And the back of the duck's head is the front of the rabbit's head!" Max added.

The professor nodded and scratched notes on his paper. "Interesting," he murmured.

"I see it, too," Luis said slowly. "It's so cool, the way the two pictures blink in and out of each other."

Ethan grinned as heads nodded throughout the room. Uri grunted, jumping up and down. Atom pointed his wing feathers at the poster and cawed, "Bunny, bunny, bunny, awk!"

"Where? Who said that?" Mr. Klumpp demanded.

He stared at the poster from every possible angle. Finally, the custodian clomped to the front of the classroom and stood right in front of the poster. His face was so close to the image that his eyes crossed.

"Nope," he said, rubbing the top of his shiny bald head. "I still don't see it."

The whole class began to giggle. The back of Mr. Klumpp's neck turned beet red.

"Ahem. Oh, yes, I see it now," the custodian said. But when he straightened up, his expression was cockeyed and confused.

"Can't even see straight," he mumbled. He stumbled toward the door, blinking.

"Mr. Klumpp," Ethan said. "Are you all —"

Thunk! The custodian walked smack into the solid wood door frame.

"Mr. Klumpp! You're hurt!" Ethan cried, leaping toward him.

"Stay away!" Mr. Klumpp sputtered. He pulled a handkerchief from his pocket and pressed it against his nose to stop the bleeding.

"Worse than a minefield in here," he grumbled as he stormed from the classroom. "Oughta be a law against it. . . ."

For the rest of the science period, Mr. Klumpp lingered in the hall outside. He rubbed his swollen nose and stared through the classroom doorway at the poster inside. "Show yourself, you wretched rabbit," he said to himself. "I know you're in there!"

CHAPTER 6

Eye Twisters

"Bloodstains everywhere, what a mess!" Mr. Klumpp kept up his muttering as he swabbed a mop across a trail of small dark-red splatters on the hall floor. "It's Flask's fault. Optical illusions, science tricks. He's a tricky one, all right!"

"Mr. Klumpp! Just the man we need!" Mrs. Ratner called out.

She darted into the hallway, grabbed Mr. Klumpp's arm, and pulled him into the book fair in the gym. She didn't let go of his shirtsleeve until they reached the sunshine that flooded the last row of bookcases, near the windows. Mrs. Ratner gave the custodian a gentle push toward four parents standing there.

"See?" she said to the amused parents. "With Mr. Klumpp we have five shadows. Five shadows for five people. Just as it should be. Then why were there only four shadows when Professor von Offel was here?"

"Five shadows," Mr. Klumpp confirmed, counting with his finger. "I can see them all right. Nothing wrong with my eyes at all."

He stepped away as Mrs. Ratner dragged yet another person into the sunlight.

Halfway back to the hallway, the custodian passed one of the book fair displays. A dizzyingly geometric book cover caught his attention. He blinked half a dozen times before he could focus enough to see the title.

"*Eye Twisters*, eh?" he read.

Mr. Klumpp opened the book and flipped through it. By the time he reached the middle pages, his eyes were crossed and his head ached.

"Why can't I see those twisters?" he wondered aloud.

He tossed the book back into the display and huffed out of the room. "Forget about it," he told himself. "Don't even think about it."

One minute later, Mr. Klumpp was standing at the front of the science lab with his eyes glued to the poster. "Where's that wily rabbit? Everybody else can see it. Why can't I?" His head was spinning.

The custodian stepped backward to get a better look. His right foot landed in his mop bucket of cold, slimy water; the bucket slid out from beneath him.

"Nooo!" he cried.

Mr. Klumpp toppled backward, arms flailing. He hit the floor backside first, landing in a lake of grimy brown water that spread slowly across the lab.

At that very same moment, Alberta, Luis, and Prescott were in the school parking lot, crouched behind Principal Kepler's shiny white hatchback.

"Did he leave yet?" Alberta asked.

"Not yet," said Luis, shaking his head.

Prescott glanced around nervously. "I'm not cut out for this stakeout stuff," he said. "What if Professor von Offel sees us? I'm barely passing science as it is."

"He's not our teacher. Mr. Flask is," Alberta pointed out. "Which, by the way, is why we decided to follow Professor von Offel in the first place, remember? We want to make sure Mr. Flask gets the Vanguard Teacher Award."

Prescott winced. "After today, I wouldn't count on it. Professor von Offel was pretty hard on Mr. Flask."

"So it's more important than ever for us to find out something about the professor's own scientific work that will help Mr. Flask impress him," Alberta insisted. "Even if that means sneaking around."

"Shhh!" Luis hissed. "There he is!"

The front door of the school swung open, and Professor von Offel stepped into the afternoon sunshine. Atom looked like a green splotch perched on the shoulder of his long black coat.

"We can still forget this whole thing," Prescott

whispered. "What if he's driving? We'll never be able to keep up."

"Calm down, Prescott. We won't get caught." Luis flicked a thumb in the professor's direction. "How could we? That guy is so out of it he wouldn't notice us if we were right on top of him."

Alberta's forehead wrinkled into a frown as she stepped out from behind Dr. Kepler's car. "Come on, guys. He's already half a block ahead. It looks like he's heading toward town." She shot Prescott a triumphant glance. "On foot."

"I know I'm going to regret this," Prescott moaned.

Luis squinted at the professor's rumpled form up ahead. "Check it out. Professor von Offel hardly says a word in class. But look at how he's waving his arms around now. Doesn't it look like his lips are moving, too?"

"A fascinating scientific mind like his." Alberta sighed. "Don't you wish we could hear what he's saying?"

"Who's he saying it to? The parrot?" Prescott shoved his hands into his pockets. "How crazy is that?"

"He's probably working out a major scientific idea," Alberta guessed. "Why didn't we plant a microphone in his briefcase?"

Some fifteen yards in front of the professor, railroad crossing lights flashed. The high-pitched blast of a train whistle sounded from a distance, followed by a chugging that grew steadily louder.

"Uh-oh." Alberta looked around, then jogged over to a garage on the side of the road. "We'd better drop out of sight until that train passes."

The railroad safety barriers descended amid a loud clang of warning bells.

"Von Offel's walking right past the gates!" Prescott cried.

Like a shot, the train streaked across the railroad crossing. The roar of its engine was deafening. A piercing whistle made all three kids jump. Even from half a football field away, they could feel the blast of heat from the train.

Yet the professor kept ambling toward the tracks as if a train crossing were no more dangerous than a field of dandelions.

"Professor von Offel! Stop!" Alberta screamed. Her cry was swallowed up by the thunderous screeching of train wheels.

"Nooo!" Luis cried.

At the last minute, Atom launched himself off the professor's shoulder and soared over the train with wildly flapping wings.

Then Professor von Offel walked right into the speeding engine.

CHAPTER 7

Vaporized!

"Ugh! Oh, my gosh. We've got to get him to the hospital!" Alberta cried.

"Or what's left of him," Prescott added.

They took off after Luis, who was already racing toward the train. He reached the crossing just as the last car rumbled past. When the gates lifted, Luis ran onto the tracks, whirling around while he tried to catch his breath.

"Wait — a — minute. Where is he?"

Prescott and Alberta were right behind him. They scanned the tracks for a long time before either of them spoke.

"There's no sign of the professor. None," Prescott finally said.

"He's gone." Alberta's dark eyes were filled with horror. "Do you think he got vaporized?"

"Vaporized! People don't just disappear into thin air," Prescott wailed.

"Even when they've been hit by a train?" Alberta wondered.

"No way. The train must have carried Professor

von Offel" — Luis gulped — "I mean, his body, away with it. There'll probably be some story about a gruesome train accident on the news."

They ran practically all the way to Alberta's house, then impatiently surfed the channels until the local news came on at five o'clock. They watched every minute, from the opening coverage of a water-main break to the final report on their minor league baseball team losing yet another game.

"Not a single word about a train accident or Professor von Offel," Luis murmured. "But it happened! We saw it with our own eyes!"

He flicked off the TV, then frowned at the blank screen. "Didn't we?"

Luis, Prescott, and Alberta held an emergency meeting at Prescott's locker on Wednesday morning.

"There wasn't anything on the news about a train accident this morning, either," Luis said. "But people are definitely going to wonder when Professor von Offel doesn't show up. We've got to say something to Mr. Flask!"

"Like what?" asked Preston. "'By the way, we just happened to see your evaluator for the Vanguard Teacher Award get vaporized by a train yesterday when we were following him?' Do you know how crazy that —"

Prescott froze. "Professor von Offel!" he gasped.

Alberta and Luis whirled around and gaped. The professor strolled down the corridor toward them, Atom perched on his shoulder.

"You're here!" Relief flooded Alberta's face as she flew toward the professor.

The professor came to a stop and squinted at them through his monocle. "Naturally, I'm here. Where else would I be?" he said impatiently.

"But yesterday" — Prescott touched the professor's sleeve, as if he couldn't quite believe it was real — "that train. It was going so fast, and you —"

"You walked right into it!" Luis finished. "We saw you. How did you survive?"

The professor's eyes had started to wander. He blinked a few times to bring them back into focus.

"Nonsense!" he said, with a wave of his hand. "I was across the tracks well ahead of the locomotive."

"It sure didn't look like it," Alberta said, biting her lip.

"Ah, well," the professor said. "We all know appearances can be deceiving."

With that, he gave a stiff bow and walked off down the hall.

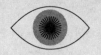

CHAPTER 8

The Walking Wounded

Luis looked up expectantly as Alberta took her seat in science class on Friday morning. "Did you get a look at his notes?" he asked.

Alberta plunked down her backpack, then shot a glance toward the professor's desk at the back of the room.

"I couldn't make out his writing," she said. "It's kind of messy."

"Kind of?" Prescott's eyebrows shot up. "I bet Uri has neater handwriting!"

Luis thrummed his fingers thoughtfully against his desk. "Professor von Offel has been writing like crazy all during Mr. Flask's classes. But he won't talk to us. And after school he shuts himself up in his office," he said. "I bet you're right about him working on something big."

"Are you saying you don't think he's a crackpot?" Alberta asked.

"He's a von Offel, which means he's definitely a crackpot," Luis insisted. "But we still need to find out more about him so we can help Mr. Flask. So far we've bombed out."

"It's not like we haven't had other stuff to do," Prescott pointed out. "We had that English quiz first period. And Mr. Flask has been keeping us pretty busy with all this optical illusion stuff."

"Good morning, everyone!" Mr. Flask called as he walked into the room in his lab coat. "Let's work in groups today. Lab assistants, can you help me get things organized?"

"You got it, Mr. Flask," Luis said. As he jumped up, he whispered to Alberta and Prescott, "We're not giving up."

"Can I pick this up? No sweat, Mr. Flask," said Sean. "Who wouldn't want to pick up a twenty-dollar bill?"

"Ah, but there's a catch here, Sean," said Mr. Flask. "Prescott will explain the rules to you."

Mr. Flask handed Heather a pair of 3-D glasses. "Okay, Alberta. You can set up the first image card now."

"It's totally blank. There's nothing to look at," Heather said as she gazed at the white card.

Mr. Flask's eyes sparkled. "Try it with the glasses on, Heather," he explained. "Remember, the red lens on one side of the glasses will absorb red rays of light, while the blue-green lens on the other side absorbs blue-green light."

"Which means that what we see with the glasses

on will be different from what we see with the naked eye." Alberta put on her own glasses, then laughed. "'Science rules'? Pretty clever message, Mr. Flask."

"I thought it was worth spreading," Ethan said, smiling. "Now —"

He breezed around the room, checking each group. "Sean, science tricks are different from optical illusions. In this case it's not your eye that is tricked but your brain. Something that seems so simple isn't. I'll give you one clue: gravity."

"I'm not giving up," said Sean. "I *will* pick up that twenty-dollar bill," he added, right before he almost landed on Prescott.

"Is your group all set up, Luis?" Mr. Flask asked.

"Sure thing, Mr. Flask. We're ready to spin."

"Spinning makes me dizzy," Max whined.

"You won't be the one rotating," said Mr. Flask.

He stopped talking as the door opened and Mr. Klumpp came in. The custodian's left ankle was taped with an Ace bandage, and he held a fluorescent lightbulb in his hand. He limped forward, looking around wildly with red-rimmed, bloodshot eyes.

"I don't believe any of our lights are out, Mr. Klumpp," Ethan told him. "You just replaced one yesterday. And another one the day before, if I recall correctly."

"And none of those looked burned out in the first place," Prescott muttered.

"You never know when the next one will blow,"

said the janitor. But he didn't even glance at the lights.

Mr. Klumpp moved toward Luis's group, his eyes on the spinners. "I know I'll see this optical illusion," he said.

Mr. Flask tried unsuccessfully to steer the custodian away. "Are you sure you want to try? I mean, after what happened to your nose and ankle . . . and your eyes seem to be a little strained."

"I can do it!" Mr. Klumpp insisted.

Luis made room for the custodian. Mr. Klumpp stared at the spinner until his eyes bulged. "It's all becoming a blur! I've had it! These illusions are illusions!" he cried. A vein pulsed on the custodian's forehead. His neck and face were bright red as he snatched his fluorescent lightbulb from the table and stormed out the door.

Mr. Flask shook his head as he watched the janitor go. "He really should see Nurse Daystrom. Okay, back to work, everyone. We'll share our results in another ten minutes."

Four springy strides took Mr. Flask to the experiment table at the front of the room, where he looked out at the class with pleasure. His tricks and optical illusions unit had turned them all into eager and curious young scientists. Surely his evaluator from the Millennium Foundation had noticed the class's enthusiasm, too?

"Professor?" Ethan stepped to the back of the classroom, where the professor sat hunched over

34

his desk, taking notes. "Do you have any questions?"

Professor von Offel didn't look up. In fact, he was so busy scratching out notes with his quill pen that he didn't appear to have heard Ethan at all. The professor stared stonily through his monocle at the messy pile of ink-smudged notes that had been growing steadily since the unit on optical illusions began.

"I do hope you'll, um, let me know if there's anything I can do for you," Ethan said.

The professor kept writing.

"Well, then —" With a sigh, Ethan retreated to the front of the class.

Perhaps the professor was concentrating so intently on his own notes that he didn't hear me, Mr. Flask thought. Or maybe he's hard of hearing.

Or maybe he doesn't like my teaching.

Ethan shook himself as Sean called out, "Mr. Flask? Is Uri supposed to look at the 3-D images, too?"

"Absolutely," Ethan said. "I thought it would be interesting to see whether Uri experiences optical illusions the same way we do."

"Whoa!" Alberta, still wearing her 3-D glasses, shrank back in her chair. "That dinosaur looks like it's coming right out of the screen at us. Hey!"

She jumped as Uri leaped behind her chair. The orangutan cowered there, grunting loudly as he clung to Alberta's arm.

"See that? Uri is trying to get away from the dinosaur, too," Mr. Flask said, calmly extracting the orangutan from Alberta's chair. "His reaction indicates that he sees the illusion as a threat."

"What about Atom?" Heather wanted to know. "Parrots are pretty smart, too, right?"

"Parrots are more intelligent than most animals. Still —" Ethan shot a dubious glance at Atom, who was perched on the edge of a glass cage at the front of the lab. "There are some exceptions. Atom arouses a peculiar reaction from the other animals."

As he spoke, a threatening hiss came from the cage. Atom took off with a squawk. He flew to the center of Luis's group and was immediately tangled up in spinner string.

"Awwk!"

"As for whether he recognizes optical illusions —" Shaking his head, Ethan untied the parrot. "Regrettably, Atom seems to lack the native intelligence."

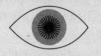

CHAPTER 9

The Stakeout

"Mr. Klumpp, would you come in here, please?"

Dr. Kepler regarded the custodian with concern as he limped into her office, rubbing his temples.

"Nurse Daystrom tells me you're suffering from chronic headaches and dizziness," said the principal. "Is this true?"

Mr. Klumpp groaned miserably.

"I'll take that as a yes," said Dr. Kepler. She jumped up to steady the custodian as he blinked and stumbled sideways. "Frankly, I'm worried about you, Mr. Klumpp. Mr. Flask says he finds you in the science lab at all hours, staring at the optical illusions he's working on with his class."

The custodian cracked open one eye, then winced and shut it again. "A man's got to do his job," he said weakly.

"The PTA is complaining, too. Something about a book you've been staring at. *Eye Twisters*?" The principal leaned back in her chair. "It looks like you've been working too hard, Mr. Klumpp. We all appreciate your dedication, but maybe you should take a few days off."

The custodian's head was still throbbing when he stumbled out of the principal's office a few minutes later. Students swarmed past him on their way to final period classes. Their voices pounded against the inside of his skull like jackhammers.

"That was so cool the way Uri could see the 3-D optical illusion," an exceptionally piercing voice spoke up behind him.

"What?" Mr. Klumpp whirled around, then grabbed his head to subdue the pain. He stood there wincing until Max and Sean were well past him down the hall.

"Impossible," he breathed. "If some oversized chimp can see those optical illusions, so can I!"

The custodian clenched his teeth, then stormed off down the hall. "No one tells George Klumpp when to work," he declared. "Or when not to work."

At the end of the school day, the lab assistants met in the hall.

"I can't believe I let you guys talk me into spying on Professor von Offel again," Prescott said to Alberta and Luis. "Didn't we learn our lesson the first time?"

"We can't give up until we know more about him," Luis insisted. "Don't forget, he's a von Offel. Another awful von Offel."

"Another brilliant von Offel," said Alberta, her eyes sparkling with intrigue. "All those notes he's been taking. I can't wait to find out what he's working on. Something really important, I bet. Like Rula von Offel's studies on evaporation. Or Colin von Offel's brain transplant work."

"Colin von Offel died trying to put his brain into a wildebeest!" Luis hissed. "And didn't Rula von Offel just disappear into thin air right in the middle of one of her so-called studies?"

"Could you guys argue about this some other time?" Prescott said. He jumped half a foot in the air as a figure in a dark suit came around the corner toward them. "Oh! Hello, Mr. Kondrakos."

The English teacher regarded them stiffly. "I should think you three students would be studying rather than gallivanting around here," he said.

"We were, ah, just coming to find out our scores on today's quiz," Alberta said.

"Why are you young people always so impatient?" Mr. Kondrakos grumbled. "In my day, students showed more respect."

"You mean back when dinosaurs roamed the earth?" Luis said under his breath.

Mr. Kondrakos cupped his hand behind his ear. "What was that, Mr. Antilla?"

"I said we'll do our best to remember that from now on," Luis said. "Sorry, Mr. Kondrakos."

Prescott wilted with relief as their teacher stepped past them. "That was close."

"Don't think I'm forgetting those cracks you made about the von Offels, Luis," Alberta whispered, tugging the strap of her backpack higher on her shoulder. "Even if they did make a few miscalculations —"

"Miscalculations? Don't make me choke. They were gross, unscientific errors!"

"Guys! Mr. Flask is the one we're supposed to be helping," Prescott pointed out. "We all agree about that, right?"

Alberta and Luis looked at each other, then nodded.

"Right," Alberta said.

She rounded the corner and tiptoed up to the closed door of the office Dr. Kepler had given Professor von Offel to use. Luis and Prescott crouched down next to her, and they peeked through the window that filled the top half of the door.

"Bingo," Luis whispered.

Professor von Offel sat behind his desk with his quill pen in his hand. Several sheets of notes lay scattered in front of him, covered with an angular, ink-splattered scrawl. The professor examined them through his monocle while Atom paced the desk in front of him.

"That writing," Luis murmured, squinting. "It looks familiar."

"Shhh!" Prescott warned.

They ducked as the professor put down his monocle and rubbed his eyes. When they looked again,

Professor von Offel was leaning back in his swivel chair with his eyes closed.

"Oh, yeah. We're going to learn a lot here," Prescott whispered sarcastically. "He's taking a nap!"

"That's not all he's doing," Alberta hissed, grabbing Prescott's arm. "Do you guys see what I see?"

Luis and Prescott looked again — then blinked.

"No way!" Prescott whispered.

Luis shook his head. "It can't be —"

As they watched, the professor's face faded slowly from sight. His hands, resting in his lap, seemed to lose their substance. For several seconds, he flickered in and out like a faulty lightbulb.

Then, all at once, there was nothing behind the desk but an empty, fading suit.

CHAPTER 10

An Out-of-Body Experience

"He's invisible!" Alberta whispered.

A loud squawk sounded from inside the office. Flapping green wings blocked her vision, and a voice said, "Hey! Scram — I mean, awk!"

Atom's sharp beak rapped loudly against the window, startling the sixth graders back a few steps. By the time they recovered their footing, the office door swung open.

"P-Professor von Offel," Prescott stammered.

The professor stood in the doorway, fully visible once more. Atom, still squawking, flapped back and forth above the desk behind him.

"What is the meaning of this?" Professor von Offel demanded.

Prescott bit his lip. "We, uh —"

"You were invisible!" Luis blurted out.

"Your hands and face totally disappeared," Alberta added, "and your suit faded." She looked at the professor in awe. "How did you do that?"

For one brief moment, the professor merely stared at them. Then he threw back his head and cackled. "Isn't it obvious?"

Alberta, Luis, and Prescott just stood there, staring blankly.

"Come now! Your class has been studying optical illusions. You three must not have been paying proper attention," the professor continued.

Alberta looked crestfallen. "Excuse me?"

"It was a simple trick of the light," the professor explained, gesturing with one hand. "Because I was sitting in front of the window."

"A trick of the light? Give me a break!" Luis scoffed. He pulled Alberta and Prescott to a stop as soon as they were out of earshot of the professor's office. "People don't just wink out that like that. The guy's not human!"

"Sure, it looked pretty weird, but" — Alberta plucked distractedly at the hem of her shirt — "maybe it was just an optical illusion, like he said."

"No way," Prescott said firmly. "Mr. Flask explained optical illusions. We know what they do. And they can't make someone fade in and out of the world. It's like the professor's a — a *ghost* or something!"

"Oh, my gosh," Luis cried. "That's it!"

"What's it?" Alberta asked. "You don't seriously think —"

"He's a ghost. He has to be!" Luis cut in. "If he's really a ghost, that would explain why he doesn't

43

know anything modern. It's because he's been dead for a long time."

"Guys, what you're saying is totally unscientific. It's insane!" Alberta grabbed Luis's arm and said, "Read my lips: There's — no — such — thing — as — ghosts!"

"Oh, yeah? That's not what Johannes von Offel thought," Luis countered. "Remember our little trip to the library?"

Alberta frowned. "There's not a single word in von Offel's *Book of Scientific Observations* about ghosts," she said. "I would have remembered it."

"Well, do you remember this?" Luis crossed his arms over his chest and quoted, "'There's no such thing as no such thing.'"

CHAPTER 11

A Ghost with a Plan

"Out of all these books, there's got to be at least one about ghosts," Luis said.

He turned down the final aisle of the school book fair, with Prescott and Alberta right behind him.

"We've already been through biography, chapter books, picture books, and history." Alberta counted the categories on her fingers. "Anyway, I still say you're on the wrong trail. Professor von Offel is not a ghost."

"Here! Scientific phenomena," Luis announced.

Prescott groaned when he saw Sean standing in the aisle right in front of them.

"Hey, what's in this section?" Sean called.

"Do I need this?" Prescott said to himself. "Isn't being in trouble with a ghost enough for one day?" He stepped in front of Luis so Sean wouldn't see the section sign. "Uh, nothing, Sean. Just books about how to do your homework."

"Bor-ing!" Sean said and walked away.

"Check this out." Luis grabbed a book and read the title. *"The Supernatural Who's Who."*

"See if it says anything about a special kind of ghost that can walk through a train," Prescott urged. He looked over Luis's shoulder, then pointed. "What about this one? Doesn't he look like Professor von Offel? They have the same hair!"

Luis shook his head. "It says this ghost is a howler," he said. "Professor von Offel hardly ever even talks, and he isn't very loud. But he might be a poltergeist who's haunting our school."

"You guys are really grabbing at straws," Alberta said. "Count me out, okay?"

She walked to the end of the aisle, where Mr. Klumpp had his whole face buried in *Eye Twisters*.

"I *will* see the illusions," the custodian chanted. "I'll do it, I'll do it, I'll do it, even if it takes me until the end of the school year!"

Meanwhile, at the other end of the school, away from the book fair, a cheer came from the professor's office.

"I've done it, Atom!" crowed the professor, jumping up from his chair.

"I'll say," the parrot said. "Keep fading out of your body like that, and the whole school will know you're a ghost!"

The professor gave a dismissive wave. "That scene with the lab assistants was just a momentary slip."

"What about that PTA lady, Mrs. Ratner?" Atom

pressed. "She's a one-woman commando squad with a mission — finding your shadow. You think she's just going to give up?"

"Oh, yes," the professor said smugly. "That shrew will forget all her doubts about me now that I've created this ingenious device."

Atom regarded the shiny metal disc hanging from a ribbon that the professor waved in front of his beak. "A medal? That's your major brainstorm?"

"This is no ordinary medal, Atom," the professor said. "This medal contains a tiny neural sensor and light-beam projector that affect the images imprinted on the eye."

"Not with the light beams again." Atom moaned. "Didn't you learn anything from the last projector you tried, Johannes? It burned a hole clear through the side of the Flask house!"

"Oh, yes. What irony that Jedidiah's home should be affected, rather than my own," the professor said, rubbing his hands together gleefully.

"Irony!" squawked Atom. "You shined that thing right at his wall!"

"Yes, well, this projector is different," the professor insisted. "Ordinarily, the brain interprets images that are imprinted on the retina. But the neural sensor in this medal reverses the process. It takes the thoughts of the brain and changes them into images the eye can see."

"Oh, brother," said Atom.

"You never could recognize genius, you impertinent piece of poultry," the professor protested. "I'm telling you, the neural sensor in this medal reads impulses from the brain of anyone who looks at it. It then feeds the information to the projector, which uses light beams to project that image. The result is that each person will see whatever is utmost in his or her mind."

Atom groaned; the professor ignored him.

"With this medal, Mrs. Ratner will see the shadow she *thinks* is supposed to be there," he continued. "Those meddlesome juvenile delinquents will see the flesh and blood of the representative from the Millennium Foundation." The professor hung the medal around his neck, then stomped toward the door.

"Mark my words, Atom. Our troubles are over!"

CHAPTER 12

Be Careful What You Wish For

The professor was halfway down the hall when Mr. Delaney, the social studies teacher, stepped out of his classroom.

"Okay," Atom said quietly in the professor's ear. "Let's see this two-bit tin medal in action."

"Shhh!"

Straightening up, the professor gave Mr. Delaney a quick nod. "Good afternoon," he said as he flashed the medal at the teacher.

"Yes, and a good afternoon to —"

All of a sudden, Mr. Delaney's mouth dropped open. "M-Mr. President! I'm s-speechless," he stammered. "To have our country's commander in chief visit our humble school —"

He bowed deeply. "May I?" Mr. Delaney grabbed the professor's hand and pumped it. Then he turned to Atom and shook his green-feathered wing. "Mrs. President, you honor us with your presence."

"Back off, pal!" screeched Atom.

He yanked his wing free, then pushed the professor down the hall, leaving Mr. Delaney to gape after them.

"See?" the professor whispered triumphantly. "He thinks I'm the President of the United States!"

"What does that make me, the First Bird?" Atom said, preening his feathers back into place.

"This promises to be quite amusing!" the professor chortled, moving forward with a lighter step. "I can't wait to see the look on Mrs. Ratner's face when —"

"Leonardo DiCaprio!" a high-pitched voice shrieked.

The professor whirled around to see a handful of girls racing toward him. They clamored around him and Atom with mooning, starstruck faces.

"We love you!" screeched one of them.

"Can I have your autograph?" cried another.

"You're king of *my* world!" said a third.

The professor jumped back as the girls pawed at his clothes. "Young ladies, please!"

On his shoulder, Atom howled with laughter. "Oh, this is good. They think you're a movie star!"

"Just get me out of here!" sputtered the professor.

"Whatever you say." The parrot beat the girls off with his wings, then squawked, "Run!"

"Phew! That was close." The professor doubled over inside the broom closet, wheezing. "The effects of my neural sensor and light projector are even stronger than I anticipated!"

"Another von Offel experiment gone totally out of whack," Atom said. "And as usual, I'm the one who has to pull you out of the mess."

"Nonsense! So far my experiment is a complete success." The professor opened the closet door a crack, looking up and down the hall. "The coast is clear," he reported. "Let's go."

They hadn't walked more than half a dozen feet when Atom murmured, "Heads up, incoming."

Mr. Kondrakos was standing in the doorway of the teachers' lounge, staring at the professor's medal. He looked up with wide, tearful eyes.

"Theo? Is that you?"

Before the professor could answer, Mr. Kondrakos threw his arms around him in a suffocating hug that knocked the wind out of the professor.

"Hey!" Atom squeezed out from beneath the big man's arms. He darted into the air as Mr. Kondrakos let out a nonstop stream of joyful exclamations in Greek.

"You were exposed to foreign languages in that circus you joined years ago," the professor gasped. "What's he saying?"

"He thinks you're his long-lost brother, Theo." Atom hovered above the two men, chuckling. "Mr. Kondrakos hasn't seen him since he left Greece forty-two years ago."

He swooped down to peck at Mr. Kondrakos's arm. "Enough, big guy! Johannes has a hard enough time staying in his body without you squeezing him out of it."

Finally he managed to pull the professor away.

"This is trouble," Atom warned as he landed on the professor's shoulder once more. "Big trouble. If you don't get rid of that crazy medal, you're going to regret it."

"Speak for yourself," the professor scoffed. "You never did have the nerve of the von Offels."

"I'm trying to save you, pal!" Atom screeched. "Lose the medal."

"No!" The professor cupped his hand protectively over the medal. "We're not done yet."

There was a demented gleam in his eye as he entered the gym a few moments later. He strode directly over to Mrs. Ratner and bowed.

"Good afternoon, madam."

"Professor von Offel! Just the man I was thinking of," Mrs. Ratner exclaimed. Grabbing his arm, she steered him through the book fair into the sunlight. "Now we can settle this business of shadows once and for all."

Atom, on the professor's shoulder, watched his own shadow floating on its own. "Uh-oh," he mumbled.

"Well, I'll be! There it is!" Mrs. Ratner shook her head in amazement, staring at the wall behind the professor. "Your shadow and your parrot's, together, just as they should be."

"Naturally," the professor said pompously, fingering the medal. "As I told you, what you saw before was nothing more than an optical illusion."

All of a sudden, he became aware of a growing crowd around him.

"Look at the clown!" cried a third-grade girl. She pointed at the professor with one hand. Her other hand clutched a book about the circus.

Next to her, a boy held a manual on dog training. "Sit, boy!" he commanded the professor. "Sit!"

"Oh, no, not HIM!" cried a fifth grader. He tossed down a copy of a Harry Potter book and stumbled backward, away from the professor. "I did not say your name! No! Get away!"

Luis took one look at the professor and dropped *The Supernatural Who's Who*.

"A poltergeist," he cried, grabbing Prescott's arm.

"A howler!" Prescott screamed. "Run!"

At the end of the row, Alberta frowned. "A ghost?" She blinked in the professor's direction. "A ghost! I guess there *is* such a thing."

Cries, shrieks, and wild laughter swelled throughout the gym. The noise level rose several decibels. Bookcases were knocked over by terrified students. Ethan and Uri, who were just entering the book fair, were pushed to the side by people scrambling for the exit.

"What —" Ethan began.

Beside him, Uri pounded his fists against his leathery chest and uttered a piercing yodel.

Alberta, Luis, and Prescott peeked out from behind a bookshelf. "That sounds familiar," Prescott murmured.

Alberta straightened up, looking out at the pandemonium-filled gym with curiosity. "Hey, did anybody else hear the mating call of the orangutan?"

CHAPTER 13

Animal Madness

"Yikes! That overgrown ape is headed this way, Johannes," squawked Atom.

"My neural sensor must work on animal brains, too!" the professor realized. "It projects the image that is uppermost in Uri's mind and —"

He broke off suddenly, shaking his head wildly back and forth. "Oh, no. It can't be! He thinks I'm —"

"His girlfriend!" Atom flapped into the air, cackling hysterically. "And it looks like he wants a kiss."

"Nooooo!" The professor darted away from Uri with an expression of sheer horror on his face.

As he barreled past Mr. Klumpp, the custodian momentarily lifted his bloodshot eyes from the geometric pattern he'd been staring at.

"Yes! Finally! I see it at last!" he shouted out, waving *Eye Twisters* triumphantly in the air. "I knew I could —"

Wham!

Uri knocked George Klumpp to the floor with the force of an eighteen-wheel tractor trailer. The orangutan pounded across the custodian's back, letting out a series of eager grunts. With a flying leap, Uri swung across an entire row of bookcases and thumped to a landing right in front of the professor.

"No — no — please!"

The professor's pleas were smothered by the orangutan's crushing hug. Ecstatic, apelike cries echoed throughout the gym. Grunting like crazy, Uri lifted the professor in his hairy arms and held him high over his head.

"Help!" shrieked the professor. "Atom, do something!"

"Let go, you amorous ape! Go eat a cold banana!" Atom swooped down and tried to beat Uri off with his wings.

At the same time, Dr. Kepler, Mrs. Ratner, Ethan, and the sixth-grade lab assistants ran up and began pulling the professor free of the ape's hairy grasp. Dr. Kepler frowned at Atom as she made a wild grab for Uri's arm.

"Did that bird just talk?"

"Awk!" Atom squawked. "Banana! Banana!"

The professor burst through the gym door to the outside, gasping for air. "I thought I'd never get away from that love-crazed ape!" he said. "I've probably got fleas all over me!"

"That's the least of your problems, Johannes." Atom took off into the air and stared past his beak at the woods surrounding the athletic fields. "Crazed canine at six o'clock!" the parrot announced.

An English terrier streaked from the woods, barking ferociously.

"Oh, no! My neural sensor is still working. That dog must think I'm a cat!" the professor cried.

He ran for the goalpost and shimmied up, kicking at the terrier. "Down. Go home, Fido!"

"Look out from above!" squawked Atom as a squadron of crows flew from the surrounding trees and dive-bombed the professor.

The professor tried vainly to pull his jacket over the medal. "I am not a worm!" he yelled. "Stop that infernal pecking!"

"Enough!" said Atom. He flapped over to the goalpost and pecked at the professor's medal with his beak. "Where's the off switch on this thing?"

"Off switch?" The professor gritted his teeth, still swatting at the crows. "What off switch?" he asked.

"You mean, there isn't one?" Atom stared at the professor in utter disbelief. "You've been dead for a hundred years, and still you never learn. For your information, it's a lot safer to invent something you can turn off!"

"You want an off switch? Fine! I'll give you one." The professor yanked off the medal and threw it on the ground. "There — it's off!"

The terrier seemed to forget all about the professor. It bared its teeth and growled at the medal while the crows pecked away at it.

"Out of the way, you mangy beasts," the professor ordered. He slid down the goalpost and stomped on the medal over and over again.

"Admit it, Johannes. You're in way over your head this time."

"That's it! I'll bury this blasted medal!" the professor cried. "Two feet should be enough to neutralize the neural sensor."

He grabbed the medal and plunged into the high-jump pit, digging frantically in the soft, deep sand.

When he was finished, the professor collapsed onto the grass, his suit and hair covered with sand.

"At last," he panted. "The panic is over."

But chaos still reigned in the gym.

"What a disaster!" Dr. Kepler picked her way slowly through the books and gift items that were strewn all over the gym floor. "Shelves knocked down, books trampled —"

She sighed, turning to the president of the PTA, who surveyed the scene in horror. "Would you mind finding Nurse Daystrom, Mrs. Ratner? Many of the students seem rather disoriented."

"It *was* Leonardo DiCaprio. It was!" A sixth-grade girl wandered past, looking into every face with searching eyes. "Where'd he go?"

Next to her, Mr. Kondrakos poked his head into the gym. "Theo? Was I hallucinating?"

"What happened?" asked Prescott as he, Luis, and Alberta stumbled through the mess. "Why was

Mr. Delaney saluting and whistling 'Hail to the Chief'?"

"I kind of went blank for a while," Luis said. He shook his head, knocking it lightly with the palm of his hand. "And then, suddenly, Uri was going crazy."

Alberta gazed thoughtfully at the orangutan, who'd been cornered by Ethan near the double doors just ahead. "What happened, Mr. Flask? It looked like Uri thought Professor von Offel was an eligible female," she said.

Mr. Flask looked puzzled. "I don't know why Uri got so excited about the professor. I guess he's not so good at identifying individuals after all." He turned to the custodian, who stood in the center of the clutter, shaking his head in disgust. "I'm very sorry about the mess, Mr. Klumpp. Ordinarily, Uri is completely docile."

"Docile, huh?" Mr. Klumpp muttered angrily. "That ape turns the entire gym upside down, and George Klumpp is left to pick up the pieces!"

"Naturally, I'll do everything I can to help clean up," Ethan offered.

Mr. Klumpp didn't appear to have heard him. Reaching down, the custodian picked up a squashed copy of *Eye Twisters* from the floor and began flipping through it.

"I saw the illusion so clearly before. I know I did." Mr. Klumpp twisted his features and wrapped the book around his face. "But now I seem to have lost the knack."

CHAPTER 14

Dinnertime

Ethan Flask brought another big bag of dried mangoes into his living room. "Have some more, Uri," he said. The orangutan was a lot calmer after having gobbled a few hearty helpings of the dried fruit. "Care to watch a little TV with me?" Ethan Flask turned on the news.

"And finally, the Einstein Elementary School track team got a slimy surprise when they landed in the high-jump pit at practice after school today."

"That's Coach Santos," Ethan sputtered.

The coach spoke into the reporter's microphone. "It was the strangest thing. My kids were hip deep in ants. Thousands of them, swarming all over some kind of weird medal."

"At least Professor von Offel can't blame that on me," Ethan murmured.

He sighed, flicking off the TV. "Still, I'm sure what happened at the book fair today is bound to color the professor's report about me to the Millennium Foundation," he groaned. "Then again, I wouldn't be the first Flask to lose a prestigious science award because of a von Offel."

Uri grunted loudly and reached into the bag for more mango.

"You're right, Uri, I guess it doesn't help to dwell on it," Ethan decided. "It's just that when there's trouble, the von Offels always seem to be nearby."

Ethan went into the kitchen to fix his dinner. He tossed a tofu pup on his solar-powered grill. Something about von Offel nagged at him as he turned over his sizzling meal.

"Professor von Offel ended up in that high-jump pit today!" he murmured. "Could he have done something to attract that army of unruly ants? No. That's too bizarre," Ethan decided. "It defies scientific methodology!" He glanced at the run-down, burned-out shell of the von Offel house next door. The professor, with Atom on his shoulder, was clearly visible through the lighted kitchen window.

"If only I could observe something concrete," Ethan said. "Some scientifically sound evidence —"

"*Now* will you listen to me?"

Atom jumped from the professor's shoulder to the scarred kitchen counter. "Thanks to your wacko medal, you almost ended up bride to the missing link! You've got to stop, Johannes!"

The professor ignored him. He was watching a

frozen dinner rotate inside a gleaming new microwave oven.

"Fascinating," he murmured. "This machine pro-
duces heat waves without the benefit of combustion
or flames. What a gloriously mad device. Worthy of
a von Offel in every way." The professor jumped to
his feet as the microwave beeped. "It's done!"

The professor jammed a giant, steaming forkful
of rice pilaf into his mouth. Atom buried his beak in
the tray of food. They both cried out in pain.

"Yeeeeow!"

Welcome to the World of
MAD SCIENCE!

The Mad Science Group has been providing live, interactive, exciting science experiences for children throughout the world for more than 12 years. Our goal is to provide children with fun, entertaining, and exciting activities that instill a clearer understanding of what science is really about and how it affects the world around them. Founded in Montreal, Canada, we currently have 125 locations throughout the world.

Our commitment to science education is demonstrated throughout this imaginative series that mixes hilarious fiction with factual information to show how science plays an important role in our daily lives. To add to the learning fun, we've also created exciting, accessible experiment logs so that children can bring the excitement of hands-on science right into their homes.

To discover more about Mad Science and how to bring our interactive science experience to your home or school, check out our website:
http://www.madscience.org

We spark the imagination and curiosity
of children everywhere!